# Reflect to Create!

## The Dance of Reflection for Creative Leadership, Professional Practice and Supervision

### Reflective Journal and Workbook

#### ELAINE PATTERSON

Reflect to *Create!*
Published and Produced 2020 by IngramSpark
Cover and text design: meadencreative.com
Editor: Emma Dickens
ISBN: 978-1-9164560-5-1

All proceeds will be gifted to help support the achievement of the 2030 United Nations Global Goal No. 4 for Sustainable Development. Global Goal No. 4 is the goal for Quality Education which is aiming to ensure inclusive and equitable quality education and promote lifelong opportunities for all by 2030. Please see www.globalgoals.org for more information.

*At the still point of the turning world.*

*Neither flesh nor fleshless;*

*Neither from nor towards;*

*At the still point, there the dance is,*

*But neither arrest nor movement.*

*And do not call it fixity,*

*Where past and future are gathered.*

*Neither movement from nor towards,*

*Neither ascent nor decline.*

*Except for the point, the still point,*

*There would be no dance, and there is only the dance.*

**T.S. Eliot from 'The Four Quartets'**[1]

**Dedicated to:**

People who work with people everywhere
who give of themselves to make the world a better place

# Welcome

*Dance is the hidden language of the soul.*
*Nobody cares if you can't dance well.*
*Just get up and dance.*
*Great dancers are great because of their passion.*
**Martha Graham**[2]

Welcome to the **Reflect to** *Create!* Reflective Journal and Workbook.

This Workbook has been designed as a companion to my first book **Reflect to** *Create! The Dance of Reflection for Creative Leadership, Professional Practice and Supervision* which was published in January 2019.

**Reflect to** *Create!* is a holistic philosophy and a manifesto for creative reflection: this is explored through the metaphor of the dance to choreograph the inner personal journeys needed to craft imaginative change for great work and inspired living in today's turbulent times. This Reflective Journal has been designed to partner with you as you dance with your questions – whatever your context. Because WHO you are, is HOW you reflect and HOW and WHAT you create.

In **Reflect to** *Create!* I define creativity as bringing the new into the world or reshaping what already exists. I define the dance of reflection and creativity as follows:

Reflection enables us to make sense and then to create meaning of our experiences of the past in the present, the present in the present and the emerging potential of the future which is already here in the present for new insights. Reflection supports us in our quest for wisdom.

Reflection is a learning process which at its best engages the subtle multi-layered, multi-dimensional faculties of our minds, bodies, hearts and souls to release or reshape what is already present or to create anew in order to develop more generative patterns of thinking, relating, doing and being which enables us – and us in our relationships with others and with our world – to survive, thrive and flourish.

This Reflective Journal and Workbook has been designed to accompany you – guiding you step-by-step – through your own creative dance to inspire reflective change and wise action. Each move and dance step for creative reflection is explained and question prompts are offered to inspire your own creative reflections.

You are invited to enter the dance wherever feels best for you. This Reflective Journal and Workbook can be used by individuals, by teams and by communities alike who want to creatively choreograph courageous conversations and elegant change for the good of all.

The **Reflect to** *Create!* body of work is based on my research, my own story, and the latest thinking in such diverse spheres as relational dynamics, mindfulness, adult learning, creativity, systems thinking, psychology, and the arts.

I would love to hear about how you are bringing **Reflect to** *Create!*'s philosophy, approach and practices alive in your work and in your life. Please do email me at Elaine@ep-ec.com with your stories, thoughts and feedforward because as Barbara de Angelis said[3]:

> The moment in between what you once were, and who you are now becoming, is where the dance of life really takes place.

May you dance!

*Elaine Patterson*

# Contents

# The *Flow*

# The *Denouement*

# The Dance

## The Reflect to *Create!* Dance and Choreography

The dance is in four moves:

*The Prelude*

*The Opening* — Retreat's Rest and Release

*The Flow* — Reflection's Fertile Void

*The Denouement* — Return's Harvest and Action

*The Prelude* is the invitation to pause and stop, the invitation to dance. Within *The Opening*, *The Flow* and *The Denouement* there are nine dance steps as shown in the illustration below. Whilst there is a natural flow and symmetry to the dance, you are also invited to step into the dance at any place and to flow backwards and forwards as you are guided by your intuition. Each move and dance step is described in the following pages.

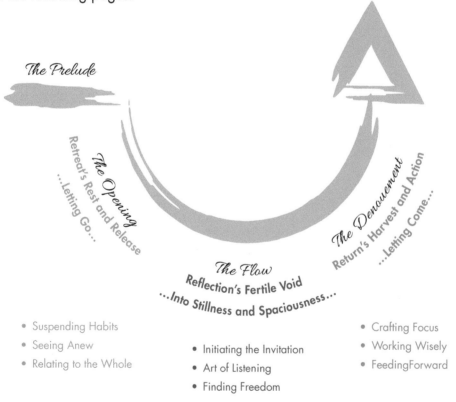

The Prelude

*The Opening*
Retreat's Rest and Release
...Letting Go...

*The Flow*
Reflection's Fertile Void
...Into Stillness and Spaciousness...

*The Denouement*
Return's Harvest and Action
...Letting Come...

- Suspending Habits
- Seeing Anew
- Relating to the Whole

- Initiating the Invitation
- Art of Listening
- Finding Freedom

- Crafting Focus
- Working Wisely
- FeedingForward

# Reflect to *Create!*'s
# Dance Partners

*Dancing is the loftiest, the most moving, the most beautiful of the arts.*
*For it is no mere translation or abstraction of life. It is life itself.*

Henry Havelock[4]

Reflect to *Create's!* dance moves and steps can be danced alone. However, there are times when we can feel ourselves getting lost or stuck in the noise. We lose our enthusiasm, flow and rhythm for the dance as well as wonder if we belong on the dance floor at all. These are times when we need a partner to dance with us.

Supervision is **Reflect to** *Create's!* dance partner. A supervisor can accompany, partner, guide, support, resource, encourage and inspire their supervisee as they explore the rhythms, tones, nuances and cadences of their practice and life for new insights, learning and change.

A Supervisor works with their practitioner to find the discordant notes, the hidden patterns, and the new choreography waiting to be revealed and worked with. A Supervisor can help find the notes which fuse WHO you are, HOW you reflect and HOW and WHAT you create. As Fiona Adamson writes:[5]

> We can step back from the action, reflecting, pondering, analysing, trying out new ways of working, getting feedback, exploring where we are vulnerable, sharing our mistakes, understanding the part that unconscious processes play in our work, learning to hold the creative tension, attending to the intuitive and imaginative parts of ourselves… being playful and experimental, allowing creative leaps and non linear transformations to emerge from the apparent chaos of the moment.

# The Prelude

# The Prelude

*Withdrawal can be the very best way of stepping forward, and done well, a beautiful freeing act of mercy. Although withdrawal can look like a disappearance – withdrawal from entanglement can precede appearing back in the world in a very real way.*

David Whyte[6]

The Prelude invites us to stop when we do not know the answer or when we need to think creatively around a question, issue or dilemma. We cannot learn if we are not prepared to make ourselves vulnerable in some way. We cannot make ourselves vulnerable without radical acts of self-compassion and self care. Chapter 4 of the book gives more background and supporting practices.

The Prelude

# Reflective Questions

Journal or draw your answers. Return to the questions as often as you need to.

**1.** What might your question be? Please note it only has to be 'good enough'. Detail and clarity will emerge as you dance with your question.

**2.** Can you feel your vulnerability physically? Where in your body do you experience it? Describe what this looks and feels like.

**3.** What generous acts of self-compassion can you gift to yourself as you dance?

# Reflective Journaling

# *The Opening*
# Retreat's Rest and Release

# *The Opening*

## Retreat's Rest and Release

*The Opening* is the sequence designed to create the space within us (and our teams)to be truly present with ourselves, with others and with our world.

*The Opening* is a sequence of three dance steps designed to help us to notice when we are 'in the grip', to redirect our attention and to open our hearts, minds and bodies to new information.

These dance steps are

Step 1   Suspending Habits

Step 2   Seeing Anew

Step 3   Relating to the Whole

- Suspending Habits
- Seeing Anew
- Relating to the Whole

# Suspending Habits

# Step 1 Suspending Habits

*While I dance I cannot judge, I cannot hate, I cannot separate myself from life. I can only be joyful and whole. That is why I dance.*

Hans Bos[7]

*Suspending Habits* encourages you to find ways to let go of what no longer serves, in order to make space for you (and your team) to tune into what wants to emerge. Letting go is a powerful inward manoeuvre to free ourselves. Chapter 5 of the book gives more background and a series of supporting practices.

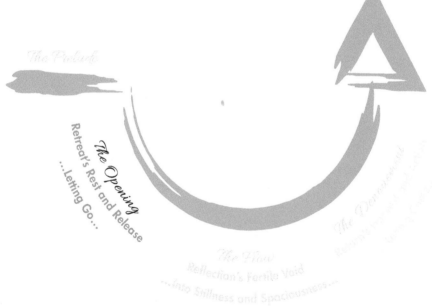

The Prelude

*The Opening*
Retreat's Rest and Release
...Letting Go...

*The Flow*
Reflection's Fertile Void
...Into Stillness and Spaciousness...

The Dénouement

- Suspending Habits
- Seeing Anew
- Relating to the Whole

- Initiating the Invitation
- Art of Listening
- Finding Freedom

# Reflective Questions

Journal or draw your answers. Return to the questions as often as you need to.

1. Ask yourself, 'What do I need to stop, suspend or let go of to open myself up to new learning here?' Give it a name. Or describe it with a metaphor. Or draw it! Befriend it as you sit with it for a while.

2. What blocks your learning here? Is it fear, judgment, cynicism or something else? Describe it. Befriend it as you sit with it for a while.

3. What permissions might you grant yourself? What support do you need to ask for here, how and from whom?

# Reflective Journaling

# Seeing Anew

# Step 2 Seeing Anew

*Originality is simply a pair of fresh eyes.*

Thomas W. Higginton[8]

*Seeing Anew* is all about learning how to be fully present, awake and alive in the moment with 'what is'. *Seeing Anew* invites us to wake up our senses, to get in touch with all that we are noticing, to open up our capacity for curiosity and wonder, to see again with fresh eyes. Chapter 6 of the book gives more background and a series of supporting practices.

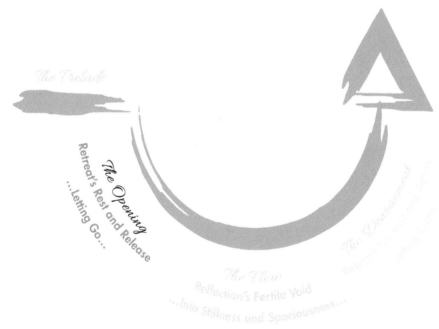

The Prelude

The Opening
Retreat's Rest and Release
...Letting Go...

The Flow
Reflection's Fertile Void
...Into Stillness and Spaciousness...

The Denouement

- Suspending Habits
- Seeing Anew
- Relating to the Whole

- Inhaling the Invitation
- Art of Listening
- Finding Freedom

# Reflective Questions

Journal or draw your answers. Return to the questions as often as you need to.

**1.** Follow the flow of your curiosity and wonder. Where is it taking you to?

**2.** What are each of your five senses – sight, hearing, touch, taste and smell – inviting you to open up to here and now?

**3.** What new ways of seeing and sensing might help here now?

# Reflective Journaling

# Relating to the Whole

# Step 3 Relating to the Whole

*Only love expands intelligence. To live in love is to accept the other and the conditions of this existence as a source of richness, not as opposition, restriction or limitation.*

Humberto Maturana[9]

*Relating to the Whole* invites us to embrace the heart's natural intelligence and innate capacities for love, relationship, connection and compassion. We can achieve a broader perspective when we shift our working from 'I' and 'me' to a deeper appreciation of 'we' and 'us' – of our shared interconnectedness, interrelatedness and humanity. Chapter 7 of the book gives more background and a series of supporting practices.

The Prelude

The Opening
Retreat's Rest and Release
...Letting Go...

The Flow
Reflection's Fertile Void
...Into Stillness and Spaciousness...

- Suspending Habits
- Seeing Anew
- Relating to the Whole

- Initiating the Invitation
- Art of Listening
- Finding Freedom

# Reflective Questions

Journal or draw your answers. Return to the questions as often as you need to.

**1.** Where are the thresholds or points of relationship and connection here for you now?

**2.** Where are the gaps and absences?

**3.** What does your heart want you to embrace or come to know?

**4.** What is your compassion and appreciation of our shared humanity inviting you to consider here?

# Reflective Journaling

# *The Flow*
# Reflection's Fertile Void

# *The Flow*

## Reflection's Fertile Void

*The Flow* is the sequence that enables us to step into the stillness and spaciousness of Reflection's Fertile Void and receive its universal, generative and creative potential.

*The Flow* is a sequence of three dance steps designed to show how we can learn to listen and receive from this vast field of emergent potential and possibility.

These dance steps are:

Step 4    Initiating the Invitation

Step 5    Art of Listening

Step 6    Finding Freedom

*The Flow*
Reflection's Fertile Void
...Into Stillness and Spaciousness...

- Initiating the Invitation
- Art of Listening
- Finding Freedom

# Initiating the Invitation

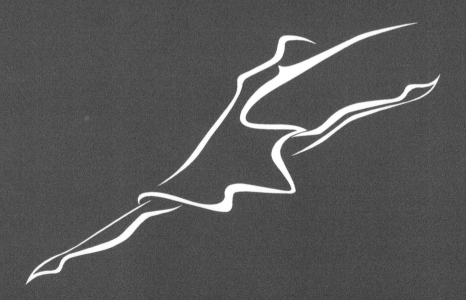

# Step 4  Initiating the Invitation

*It is only in the intentional silence of the vigil and meditation, or in the quiet places of nature that we encounter the song of the universe.*

Caitlin Matthews[10]

*Initiating the Invitation* enables us to create the space within ourselves to step into the unknown and access its creativity and potential (which cannot be forced or commanded into action). This is the art of losing ourselves in order to become fully present to not knowing and to being in the unknown. Chapter 8 of the book gives more background and a series of supporting practices.

*The Flow*
Reflection's Fertile Void
...Into Stillness and Spaciousness...

- Initiating the Invitation
  - Art of Listening
  - Finding Freedom

# Reflective Questions

Journal or draw your answers. Return to the questions as often as you need to.

**1.** What is your invitation to yourself here?

**2.** Can you allow yourself to get lost in order to find yourself as you explore your question?

**3.** What needs to happen within you to enable you to sit with not knowing until something new or reshaped arrives?

# Reflective Journaling

# Art of Listening

# Step 5  Art of Listening

*Inner guidance is heard like soft music in the night*
*by those who have learned to listen.*

Vernon Howard[11]

*The Art of Listening* is an act of deep respect, intimacy and humility. Learning to listen to ourselves, to others and to our world honours life. Profound listening comes from our profound presence – from a stillness, from a curiosity and from a willingness to be changed by our listening. Chapter 9 of the book gives more background and a series of supporting practices.

*The Flow*
Reflection's Fertile Void
...Into Stillness and Spaciousness...

- Initiating the Invitation
- Art of Listening
- Finding Freedom

# Reflective Questions

Journal or draw your answers. Return to the questions as often as you need to.

**1.** How are you listening?

**2.** Who and what are you listening to?

**3.** What are you listening for?

# Reflective Journaling

# Finding Freedom

# Step 6 Finding Freedom

*And the world cannot be discovered by a journey of miles, no matter how long, but only by a spiritual journey, a journey of one inch, very arduous and humbling and joyful, by which we arrive at the ground at our feet, and learn to be at home.*

From 'A Spiritual Journey' by Wendell Berry[12]

*Finding Freedom* is tuning into our intuition and allowing our inner wisdom to guide us home to ourselves. *Finding Freedom* is about accessing our integrity and wholeness as role marries soul, and as we express ourselves in the world. Chapter 10 of the book gives more background and a series of supporting practices.

The Prelude

*The Flow*
Reflection's Fertile Void
...Into Stillness and Spaciousness...

- Initiating the Invitation
- Art of Listening
- Finding Freedom

# Reflective Questions

Journal or draw your answers. Return to the questions as often as you need to.

1. How is your intuition guiding you here?

2. What does your soul want you to embrace or want you to know?

3. What is emerging for you – either in reshaping the old or in new forms?

4. What does freedom to embrace all of you who you are mean for you now? What does freedom look and feel like for you now?

# Reflective Journaling

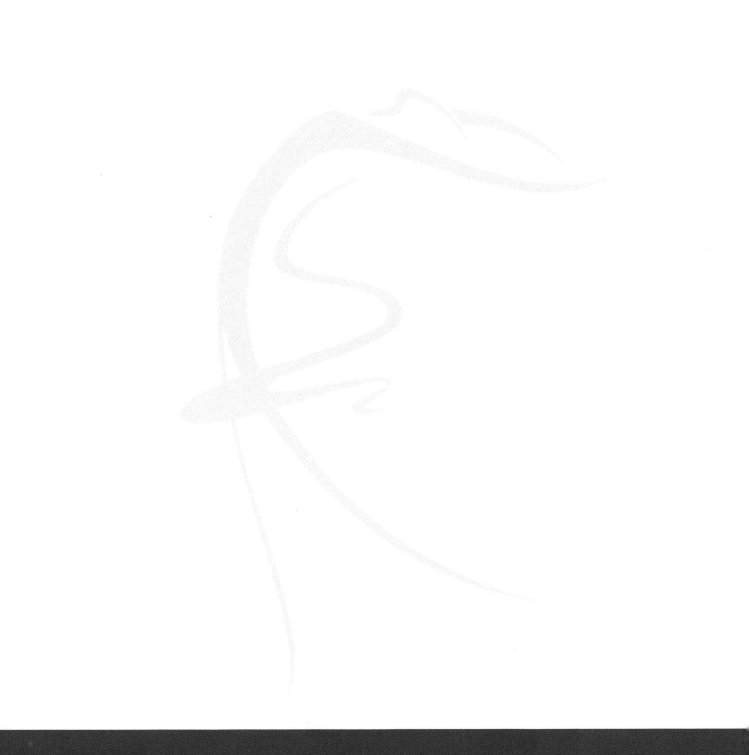

# The Denouement
## Return's Harvest and Action

# *The Denouement*

## Return's Harvest and Action

*The Denouement* is the sequence, which enables us to return to harvest, test and apply the discoveries and riches from *The Flow* to reshape what already exists or bring something new into the world.

*The Denouement* is a sequence of three dance steps where choices, options and decisions are designed, formulated, tested and applied. Here the invisible is made visible, the implicit made explicit.

These dance steps are:

Step 7    Crafting Focus

Step 8    Working Wisely

Step 9    FeedingForward

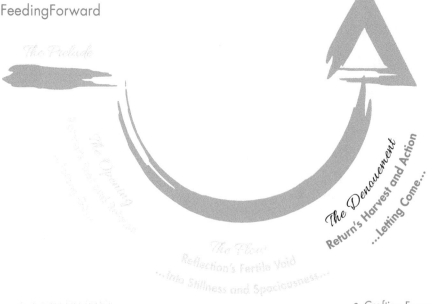

The Prelude

The Opening

The Flow
Reflection's Fertile Void
...Into Stillness and Spaciousness...

The Denouement
Return's Harvest and Action
...Letting Come...

- Inciting the Invitation
- Art of Listening
- Finding Freedom

- Crafting Focus
- Working Wisely
- FeedingForward

# Crafting Focus

# Step 7  Crafting Focus

*Focus: the point at which rays or waves meet after reflection or refraction...the point at which rays appear to proceed...converge or make convergence to a focus...the adjustment of the eye or lens necessary to produce a clear image.*

Concise Oxford Dictionary[13]

*Crafting Focus* invites us to hone, refine and clarify our discoveries from *The Flow*. It is the invitation to test and to experiment. *Crafting Focus* enables us to decide what needs to be created or reshaped and when; and is the energy for action, which creates visibility, responsibility, and accountability. Chapter 11 of the book gives more background and a series of supporting practices.

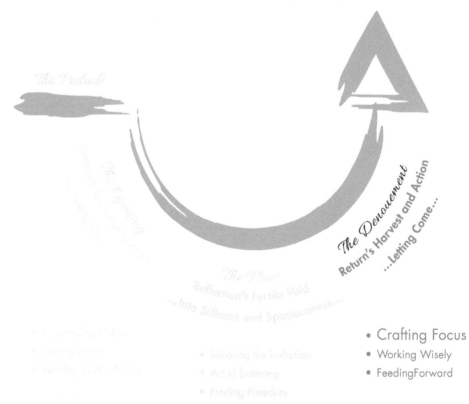

The Prelude

The Denouement
Return's Harvest and Action
...Letting Come...

The Flow
Reflection's Fertile Void
...Into Stillness and Spaciousness...

- Initiating the Invitation
- Art of Listening
- Finding Freedom

- Crafting Focus
- Working Wisely
- FeedingForward

# Reflective Questions

Journal or draw your answers. Return to the questions as often as you need to.

**1.** What options appear open now?

**2.** What is known and what needs to be tested?

**3.** What small steps to test your ideas could be taken now?

# Reflective Journaling

# Working Wisely

# Step 8  Working Wisely

*How you do one thing is how you do everything.*

Zen saying[14]

*Working Wisely* means making wise choices – and being held responsible and accountable for those choices – which are in service of you, your clients and your systems. *Working Wisely* means paying attention to the 'what' and the 'how' of making change happen. *Working Wisely* is a fine balancing act, which requires holding the system in mind as you test your ideas. Chapter 12 of the book gives more background and a series of supporting practices.

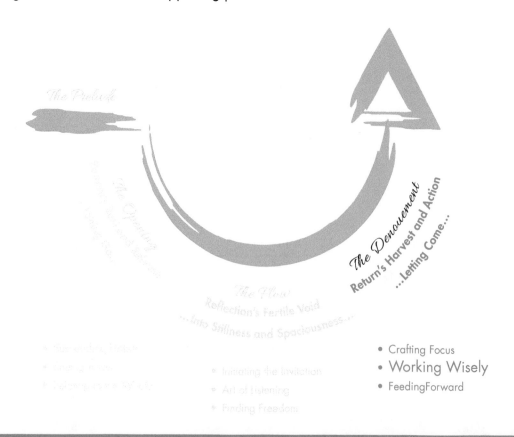

- Crafting Focus
- **Working Wisely**
- FeedingForward

# Reflective Questions

Journal or draw your answers. Return to the questions as often as you need to.

**1.** How do your options for change need to be placed and pursued? What discernment is needed here?

**2.** How will your proposed decisions or actions attend to and / or energise the wellbeing of the whole?

**3.** What trade-offs or compromises might be needed from you and / or others?

# Reflective Journaling

# FeedingForward

# Step 9  FeedingForward

*By three methods we may learn wisdom: First, by reflection, which is noblest; Second, by imitation, which is easiest; and Third, by experience, which is the bitterest.*

Confucius[15]

*FeedingForward* gives us the intelligence we need, to learn from the past in order to reshape and create in the present with wisdom and without anxiety or shame. *FeedingForward* gives us the data to show how our intention is being experienced by others. It is a navigational system, showing if and how we are on course, and what needs to be altered, adjusted or stopped. Chapter 13 of the book gives more background and a series of supporting practices

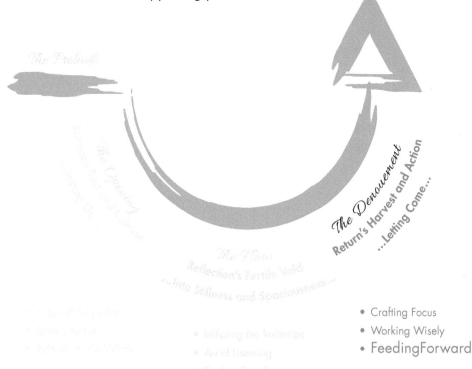

The Prelude

The Denouement
Return's Harvest and Action
...Letting Come...

The Flow
Reflection's Fertile Void
...Into Stillness and Spaciousness...

- Initiating the Invitation
- Ardent Listening
- Finding Freedom

- Crafting Focus
- Working Wisely
- FeedingForward

# Reflective Questions

Journal or draw your answers. Return to the questions as often as you need to.

**1.** What FeedForward processes do you need to put in place to stay on course?

**2.** How will you honour the FeedForward data you receive?

# Reflective Journaling

# Finding Your Feet

# Reflect to *Create!* Dance Map

## *Finding Your Feet*

*Wanderer there is no path. The path is made by walking – and by dancing. Wanderer your footsteps (or dance steps) are the road, and nothing more; wanderer there is no road, the road is made by walking. By walking one makes the road, and upon glancing behind one sees the path that never will be trod again.*

Taken and adapted from Antonio Machado, Campos de Castilla[16]

Here is a simple and easy self-assessment you can use at any time (and also any number of times) during your inquiry or project to explore where you are, what dance steps might need to be re-visited, re-freshed or re-choreographed, what is missing and what needs your focus and attention.

The Denouement

The Prelude

The Opening

The Flow

Feeding Forward

Vulnerability

Working Wisely

Gift of Self Compassion

Crafting Focus

Suspending Habits

Finding Freedom

Seeing Anew

Art of Listening

Relating to the Whole

Initiating the Invitation

Reflect to *Create!* Dance Map
Finding Your Feet

# Reflective Questions

Journal or draw your answers. Return to the questions as often as you need to.

**1.** What am I noticing?

**2.** What is emerging?

**3.** What now needs my attention?

# Reflective Journaling

# Staying in Touch

Reflect to *Create!* is a holistic philosophy and set of reflective practices designed to free your innate creativity and humanity to craft wise, compassionate and skilful leadership, professional practice and supervision.

The Centre for Reflection and *Creativity* has been established to support this work.

Different ways of staying in touch and getting on-going inspiration and support are suggested below:

**1.** Join the Reflect to *Create!* Community on Facebook at **www.facebook.com/groups/2214822445459157/about**

**2.** Visiting my website at **www.elainepattersonexecutivecoaching.com** for my latest blogs, audios and resources which also includes our range of Reflect to *Create!* journals, pens, prompt cards and workbooks.

**3.** Follow me on LinkedIn, Instagram, Pinterest and Twitter.

**4.** Join us on our Reflect to *Create!* Workshops, Online Saloons, Learning Circles, Retreats and Practitioner Training Programmes. Visit my website or email me directly at **Elaine@ep-ec.com**. They have all been uniquely designed to deepen your appreciation of our Reflect to *Create!* philosophy, its practice and its application in your world.

# References

[1]  T.S. Eliot 1944) *Four Quartets*. Pp 15. London, Faber Paperbacks

[2]  Downloaded 10th March 2017. www.goodreads.com/quotes/tag/practice

[3]  Downloaded 17th December 2019 from www.curatedquotes.com/inspirational-quotes/dance/

[4]  Downloaded 6th February 2018 from www.curatedquotes.com/inspirational-quotes/dance/

[5]  Adamson, F. (2010) *Definitions of Supervision*. Unpublished. CSA Diploma Student Handbook

[6]  Whyte, D. (2014) *Consolations: The Solace, Nourishment and Underlying Meaning of Everyday Words*. Pp 237. Langley, Many Rivers Press

[7]  Hans Bos. Downloaded 2ndMay 2019 www.searchquotes.com/quotation/While_I_dance_I_cannot_judge%2C_I_cannot_hate%2C_I_cannot_separate_myself_from_life._I_can_only_be_joyfu/3897/#ixzz4fuMVcWvG. It was used by Landra French as the heading quote for the Sept-Oct 1995 issue of *The Crescent Moon* (Volume 2, Issue 5)

[8]  Quote downloaded 12th May 2017 from www.searchquotes.com/search/Fresh_Eyes/#ixzz4gwoNPBJV

[9]  Downloaded 16th June 2017 from www.asquotes.com/author/19933-Humberto_Maturana

[10]  Caitlin Matthews cited in Cameron, J. (1994) *The Artist's Way – A Course in Discovering and Recovering Your Creative Self*. Pp 173. London, Pan Books

[11]  Downloaded 25th September 2017 from www.goodreads.com/quotes/tag/listening?page=3

[12]  Downloaded 31st October 2017 from www.goodreads.com/author/quotes/8567.Wendell_Berry

[13]  *The Concise Oxford Dictionary*. (1976) 6th Edition. Pp. 407. Oxford, Clarendon Press

[14]  Downloaded 23rd July 2018 from lifehacker.com/the-way-a-person-does-one-thing-is-the-way-they-do-eve-1672939489

[15]  Downloaded 29th January 2018 from www.goodreads.com/author/show/15321.Confucius

[16]  Downloaded on 17th December 2019 from www.Goodreads.com

Printed in the USA
CPSIA information can be obtained
at www.ICGtesting.com
LVHW062343251223
767357LV00056B/1299